Cashmere

A COMPLETE GUIDE

FROM FIBRE TO FASHION

SUE MEECH

Illustrations by Adam Campbell

Photography by Matthew Wood

SANDY PINES PRESS

P&M WOOLCRAFT
HANDSPINNING EQUIPMENT
PINDON END
HANSLOPE
MILTON KEYNES MK19 7HN
TEL: 01908 510277 FAX: 01908 511706

Sandy Pines Farm
Sue Meech
R. R. #6 Napanee, Ontario
K7R 3L1
Canada

613-354-0264

Canadian Cataloguing in Publication Data

Meech, Sue, 1942-
  Cashmere: a complete guide from fibre to fashion.

Includes bibliographical references and index.
  ISBN 0-9680954-0-2.

1. Cashmere I. Title

TS1548.C38M44 1996   677'.33   C96-900504-0

i

ABOUT THIS BOOK

This book is a comprehensive guide to understanding and working with cashmere fibre. The author introduces the reader to the history of this unique fibre, describing the different types of cashmere bearing goats.

Cashmere classification, purchasing and storing this fibre are explained, including methods of harvesting and dehairing. Fibre washing and methods of preparation are compared and illustrated.

Handspinning cashmere and cashmere blends are explored in easily understandable terms for the novice spinner. A chapter dealing with dyeing the fleece and yarn will help to eliminate any apprehension that handspinners may feel when dealing with this expensive exotic fibre.

Working with cashmere yarn includes weaving and knitting. Patterns are provided for simple and complex projects for all levels of handspinners and knitters, so that the reader may enjoy this luxurious fibre and use the finished yarns to create a unique garment.

For the aspiring goat herder there is information on raising cashmere goats for fun and profit. A comprehensive list of resources for the fibre and the goats in Canada and the United States is included in the appendix.

From fibre to fashion, you will travel the road from the old world to the new, where natural fibres are experiencing an amazing revival in the world of fashion.

TABLE OF CONTENTS

ACKNOWLEDGEMENTS

When I first began learning about cashmere, I felt isolated, as there was so little information available. Many people have helped me gain the knowledge that I needed to raise cashmere goats, use their beautiful fibre and eventually to produce this book.

I would like to thank my husband, Donald, for all his patient support, and for cleaning out the barns, while I sat in the study being creative.

Dorothy Budge-Kirk has played an important role in the production of this book. Her enthusiasm for knowledge of anything related to handspinning has been an inspiration. She gently encouraged me to finish my Master Spinners Program and would not let me falter.

The author with her Cashmere Goats.

Thanks to Adam Campbell for his pen and ink illustrations, Matthew Wood for his photography and Kenn Morrison for his desktop publishing.

I would like to thank the membership of the Eastern Cashmere Association, especially Marilyn Merbach and Marilyn and Wes Ackley. Organizations such as the Cashmere Producers of America (CaPrA) and Cashmere America have been instrumental in the formation of this book. Through newsletters and workshops sponsored by these organizations combined with the experience gained by producing my own cashmere on my farm, I have learned all that I know about this exotic down, from fibre to fashion.

iv

FOREWORD

In 1989, on a trip to New Zealand, I noticed that the scenery had changed since I had last lived there fifteen years ago. There used to be sheep dotting the landscape wherever I travelled, now there were white animals, but they were not sheep. A closer look revealed that they were white goats that were covered with beautiful fibre. My curiosity was aroused and we chanced upon a large farm with the hillside covered with these goats. I introduced myself to the goat farmer and in turn was introduced to cashmere goats and their exotic fibre. It was love at first sight.

When I returned home to Canada, I found that there was very little information about these animals and their fibre. This was partly due to the fact that cashmere, as an industry, is relatively new in North America. I began my search for information about the animal and cashmere fibre, which led to a very exciting few years gathering data all over North America.

The next step was to produce my own cashmere, so I began importing goats from the U.S.A. that had origins from Australia and Spain. As I was completeing my final year at Georgian College, working on a Master Spinners Certificate, I decided to make cashmere fibre the subject of my in-depth study, to document the information I had obtained.

With that objective reached, I began to plan this book, so that I could share this information with other fibre enthusiasts. I hope that armed with this knowledge, the reader will enjoy working with cashmere as much as I do.

THE HISTORY OF CASHMERE

The history of fibre producing goats is long, possibly dating back as far as the beginning of mankind. The wild goats probably originated in Asia and were the ancestors of the domestic goats that we know of today. At some point in their long evolution, they developed the underwool of down in order to survive harsh environments. They have endured and evolved as strong animals that can live where others cannot, in cold mountainous areas of the world, where the grazing is marginal.

There are three basic kinds of goat fibre:
hair - which is the outer coarse fibre only
cashmere - which is the fine down
mohair - which is similar to sheep fleece, with all the fibres of similar diameter.

Cashgora is a relatively new fibre, originating from the crossing of down bearing goats with the Angora, mohair producing goats. This crossing improved the fineness of the mohair on the Angora goat and made the dominant colour white in cashmere bearing goats. This has caused problems with the coarsening of some of the cashmere coming from stock raised in Australasia. Some of the goats imported from these countries carry the genes for mohair, which causes the production of an intermediary fibre that is not removed during the dehairing process.

Some believe that the origin of these animals dates back to the early days of the Spanish Armadas. Sailors would take goats with them for fresh food and realising the possibility of shipwrecks, left a few goats behind on many of the islands. If a wreck occurred, they would then be able to survive, with meat and dairy produce available. These hardy animals not only survived but multiplied quickly, sometimes ruining the ecological balance on the islands as they ate along river banks, causing erosion and browsed on the young trees.

There is a long history of cashmere hair, the thick outer protective coat of the animal, being used for cloth and carpets in Asia. The cashmere fleeces were also used for weaving cloth for making tents for the nomadic herdsmen, who travelled with their goats seeking new pastures.

THE HISTORY OF CASHMERE *(cont'd)*

Cashmere fibre is the under down of the domestic goat of central Asia and the goats which are now raised in North America. These goats moult once a year, in the Spring in the wild, unlike Angora goats that have had that tendency bred out of them by genetic selection. Cashmere goats come in many colours, white, grey, brown and black. They may be solid coloured or multi-coloured, with the colour of the guard hair often bearing little relationship to the colour of the down.

With natural fibres increasing in popularity in the fashion world, new interest in cashmere fibre is occurring in many areas of the world. This unique, exotic fibre is getting the recognition it deserves at long last.

CHINESE CASHMERE

There are millions of cashmere bearing goats in China. They generally inhabit the mountainous areas where there is no agricultural land, ranging freely with their herders, seeking new grazing. Once a year they rendezvous for fleece gathering, usually done in a single combing.

Production of cashmere is estimated at 5,000 tonnes per year with an average diameter of 15 microns, which makes it valuable and highly sought after. The guard hair is consistently longer than the down, and these goats look quite different from the cashmere goats of North America. They have distinctive horns and all have long guard hair which protects the down from moulting, holding it in place until it is removed by combing.

Chinese cashmere is beautiful with no lustre and a soft hand. Research is being carried out to improve cashmere production in China, as it is a very valuable export.

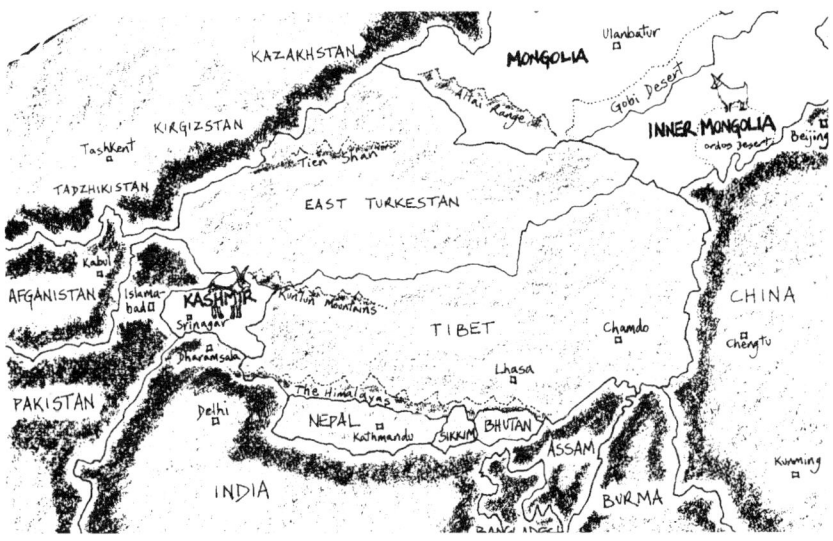

Inner Mongolia has a goat population of about four million cashmere bearing animals, producing 1,500 tonnes per year with an average down diameter of 14 microns. The fineness of the down is probably due to the harsh physical conditions of the environment and the poorer nutrition.

Dehairing plants and woollen mills are very modern in China and employ thousands of workers who process the fibre to yarn and knitted garments of excellent quality, which are then sold world wide at competitive prices.

BOER GOATS

The history of the Boer goat is centuries long and began in South Africa. Many breeds from Europe as well as Africa contributed genes to this goat, a favourite of the nomadic Hottentot tribe. Although the Boer goat is a good milk producer and raises multiple kids with ease, it has always been a multi- purpose animal, raised for its meat, milk and hide by the local tribes.

In South Africa there several types of Boer goat, but the one that has gained popularity in North America is the Ennobled breed that was originally exported from South Africa to Australasia and from there to North America. Frozen embryos were imported from New Zealand and implanted into North American does who were kept in quarantine until kidding had occurred.

At the present time there are several Boer goats being used for breeding all over North America. These Boer goats have distinctive markings, being white with a red head, ears and neck. The average weight is 63Kg. for does and 130 Kg. for bucks. They are large, sturdy animals that mature quickly, making them excellent meat goats.

Cashmere production varies from animal to animal, but the genes do exist for the secondary hair follicle that produces down, in most of these goats. Although in some Boer goats the down may be too short to be of any commercial value, if this goat is bred with a long haired cashmere goat, there is great potential for offspring to produce long, thick cashmere. The cashmere is fine, about 16 micron diameter and white because of the white body of the Boer goat.

These goats are being used across North America to reclaim land over-run with weeds and bush. This makes them a triple purpose goat: meat, cashmere producing and weed eaters. The prices of these animals has fallen to about $1000 per animal in 1996 from $20,000 a few years ago. Boer goats will soon be as popular as many other goat breeds.

CASHGORA

The term "Cashgora" is confusing to producers and spinners of this fibre. The term has several definitions and is not a universal name by any means. To some the term refers to an animal, a goat that is a cross between a cashmere goat and an Angora

A Cashgora Goat: Cashmere/Angora cross

Page 5

goat. To cashmere producers, this term means a fibre that is from a cashmere goat with down over 18 microns in diameter, causing an intermediary fibre that makes down separation difficult.

In New Zealand, this term is applied to a feral goat, with a two coated fleece with a down diameter under 22 microns in diameter, probably because the feral goats had an infusion of Angora somewhere in their past.

Cashmere producers and processors make a cut off point for fibre diameter when describing cashmere. Any fibre over 18 microns in diameter is described as cashgora. Once a fibre has reached this state, it has less crimp and higher lustre than the finer cashmere. There is a market for this fibre, but it must be processed separately to maintain the high quality required by buyers of cashmere.

Cashgora fibre is excellent for weaving yarn and blending with other fibres. The price of this fibre is usually considerably less than that of cashmere, so it is a good buy for handspinners with a weaving project in mind.

Cashgora comes in many natural colours and because of its lustre takes up dye very well. Once the fibre has been separated and all the guard hairs removed, it is difficult to realize that this is not cashmere. It is fine and soft but the lustre present in the spun yarn is easily seen. Seen under the microscope and magnified about 2000 times, the scales of the fibre can be seen to curve.

Unfortunately, cashgora has not been given the recognition that it deserves, mainly because some of it has been placed in with cashmere, bringing the prices down. It is a delightful fibre to work with and well worth a try. With its soft silky hand it reminds me of very fine mohair and it spins and washes in a similar way.

CLASSIFICATION

Understanding cashmere classification will assist the spinner to choose the correct fibre for the end use. For a baby item or a garment that is worn next to the skin, finer cashmere is preferred, but coarser cashmere or cashgora would be suitable for an outer garment. Cashmere is an expensive fibre, so knowledge about the types of fibre available will assist the spinner to get value for their money.

Fibre Type:
Cashmere is the fine dehaired down fibres produced by any breed of goat, there is no such animal as a cashmere goat. Some dairy goats such as the Saanen and Pygmy goats may carry the gene that gives rise to the down undercoat, but it is frequently too short to use for spinning.

Cashmere fibre is usually non-medullated with a maximum diameter of 18.5 microns and a minimum length of 1 1/4 inches. The down should have a consistent crimp in the fibre, have no lustre and a soft hand. Although the guard hair length may vary and be longer or shorter than the down, there should be a marked difference between the two fibres even to the naked eye.

Colour:
Cashmere is classified into colour groups.
1. *Super White:* (WW).
    Pure white with no coloured down or guard hair, with no stains that are unscourable. It commands the highest price because of its uniformity.
2. *White/Coloured:* (WC).
    Pure white fleece, with the occasional coloured guard hair. This fleece should dehair into pure white down.
3. *Grey:* (GY).
    All fleece including beige and greys.
4. *Brown:* (BR).
    All fleece from mid to dark colour.

Length and Yield:
The minimum length requirement is 33mm (1¼"). Any fibre shorter than this would be ruined in combing or shearing and make the fibre difficult to spin by hand or commercially. Shorter down fibre is frequently found on the neck or britch and should be skirted off.

CLASSIFICATION *(continued)*

There should be few second cuts when shearing and the combing should be gentle to avoid breaking any of the down fibres. Second cuts and damaged fibres will cause problems in the finished garment such as pilling and weak areas in the yarn.

Any fleece purchased should yield at least 15% down to guard hair, otherwise there would be too much waste to make this worthwhile from a cost perspective.

DOWN DIAMETER:

Diameter of the down increases with the age of the goat. The finest down comes from kid hair. A diameter of 18.5 microns or under is essential for the fibre to be classed as cashmere. The finer the micron diameter the higher the price for the down.

Cashmere Fibre

Fibre has a lot of crimp - 17 micron diameter.

Cashgora Fibre

Fibre has little or no crimp, but fine waves - 20 micron diameter, showing Mohair tendencies.

Mohair Fibre

Fibre has coarse waves - 24 micron diameter
Fine mohair, smoother fibre.

Cashmere fleeces may be sent to several companies that specialize in fibre ananlysis. The histogram gives the percentage of fibres that fall within a distinct micron range.

A HISTOGRAM OF CASHGORA FLEECE

```
10 | o··o
11 | o··o
12 | o··o-o-o ·o··o··o
13 | o··o··o··o··o··o··o··o··o··o··o··o··o··o··o··o··o··o··o··o··o
14 | o··o··o··o··o··o··o··o··o··o··o··o··o··o··o··d··o··o··o··b··o··o··o··o··o··D
15 | o··o··o··o··o··o··o··o··o··o··o··o··o··o··o··o··o··o··o··o··o··g··o··o··o··o··o··o··o··O
16 | o··o··o··b··o··o··o··o··o··s··o··s··o··o··o··o··b··o··o··o··o··o··o··b··o··o··o··o··o··o··o··o··O
17 | o··o··o··o··o··o··o··o··b··o··g··o··o··o··o··o··o··o··o··o··o··o··o··o··o··o··o··o··a··o··o··O
18 | o··o··o··o··o··o··o··o··b··o··o··o··b··o··o··o··o··o··o··o··o··o··o··o··o··o··o··o··o··o··o··O
19 | o··o··o··o··o··o··o··o··o··o··o··o··o··o··o··o··o··o··o··o··o··o··o··o··o··o··o··o··o··o··•
20 | o··o··o··o··o··•··o··•··o··o··o··o··o··o··o··O··o··o··o··o··o··o··o··o··o··o··o··o··o··o··o··O
21 | o··o··o··o··o··b··o··o··o··o··o··o··o··o··o··o··o··o··o··b··o··o··o··O
22 | o··•··o··o··•··o··o··o··o··o··o··o··o··o··O
23 | •··o··o··o··o··o··o··o··d··o··o··o··o··o··O
24 | o··o··o··•··o··o··o··o··o··•··o··•··O
25 | o··•··D··o··o··o··o··•··o··O
26 | o··o··o··•··o··O
27 | •··o··O
28 | o··•··O
```

Although some of the fibre in this fleece is cashmere, a large percentage of the fibre falls into the 19 to 25 micron range. This is intermediary fibre that appears slightly lustrous and wavy and would be harder to separate in the dehairing process.

A HISTOGRAM OF CASHMERE FLEECE

```
10 | o··o··o··o··o
11 | o··o··o··o··o··o··o··o··o··o··o··o··O
12 | o··o··o··o··o··o··o··o··o··o··o··o··o··o··o··o··o··o··O
13 | o··o··o··o··o··o··o··o··o··o··o··o··o··o··o··o··o··o··o··o··o··o··o··o··o··o··O
14 | o··o··o··o··o··o··o··o··o··o··o··o··o··o··o··o··o··o··o··o··o··o··o··o··o··o··o··o··O
15 | o··•··o··o··o··o··o··o··o··o··o··o··o··o··o··o··o··o··o··o··o··o··o··o··o··o··o··o··o··O
16 | o··o··o··o··o··o··o··o··o··o··o··o··o··o··o··o··o··o··o··o··o··o··o··o··o··o··o··o··O
17 | o··o··o··o··o··o··o··o··o··o··o··o··o··o··o··o··o··o··o··o··o··o··o··o··•··O
18 | o··o··o··o··o··o··o··o··o··o··o··o··o··o··o··o··o··o··O
19 | o··o··o··•··o··•··o··o··•··o··o··o··o··o··o··o··O
20 | o··o··o··•··o··o··o··o··o··o··o··o··o··o··O
21 | •··o··o··o··o··o··o··o··o··•··O
22 | •··o··o··o··o··o··o··o··•··O
23 | o··o··o··o··o··o··O
24 | o··o··O··o
25 | o··o··o
26 | •··o
27 | o··o
28 | o
```

This is a good fleece, with most of the cashmere fibres falling in the 13-16 micron range.

COMBED FLEECE VERSUS SHORN FLEECE:

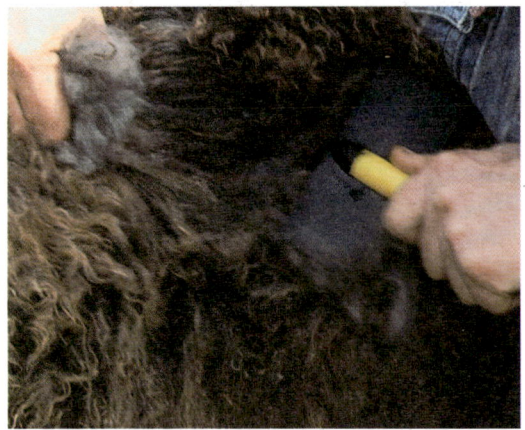

Hand combing a fleece

With combed fleece, there is less guard hair, therefore less wasted fleece. It will cost more per ounce, but will yield more down for the spinner. As long as there is little damaged fibre, this is the least expensive fleece for a handspinner to buy. There will be guard hairs to separate from the down, but not as many as in a shorn fleece.

As combed fleece is collected in the Spring when the goat begins its own natural shedding cycle, there may be dandruff present as the skin cells deteriorate and die under the thick fleece. This is usually separated in commercial dehairing, but may present more problems for the hand dehairer and spinner. With the combed

An almost completely shedded goat

fleece there is little possibility of second cuts and less concern for the goat if the weather should turn suddenly cold as it has its hair coat intact to protect it.

A partially combed goat

Large flocks of goats are usually shorn for cost effectiveness, as it takes a few minutes to shear and an hour to comb a fleece. If shearing is done early in the shedding cycle, which is January to March in North America, there is no fleece accidentally lost on the fence or bushes when the animal rubs itself to rid it of the down.

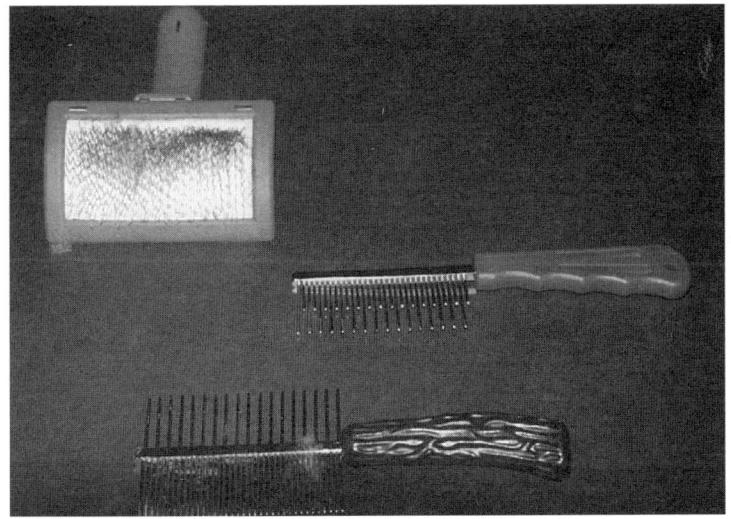
Combing Equipment

Page 11

DEHAIRING CASHMERE

Cashmere fleeces can be dehaired by hand, although this is a time consuming exercise. I have discovered two methods that are relatively easy for the hand-spinner to prepare their own fibre from the fleece, but be warned, this is a slow process!

i) Take a small lock of the fleece, fold it over into two, length-wise, allowing the guard hairs to spring out from the down, making it easy to remove them.

ii) Cashmere can be more easily separated from the guard hair when it is wet. Submerge small amounts under luke-warm water. This can be done using a sieve with the fleece placed in it. This enables submersion and removal of the fleece from the water with virtually no handling of the fibres. The guard hairs will stand up out of the down and can be removed relatively easily. If the fleece is dirty, a small amount of liquid soap such as Ivory can be used to scour the fleece at the same time.

Commercially prepared down has already been scoured before dehairing and needs no further washing before it is spun. Dehairing is a highly technical process and the exact method is kept a secret. The main dehairing plant in North America is the Forte Cashmere Company, Woonsocket, Massachusetts.

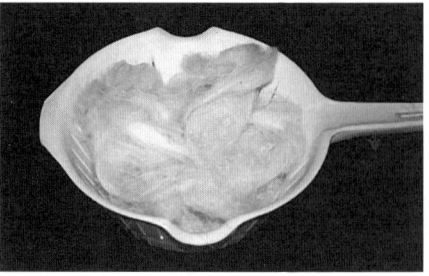

A sieve full of fleece for washing

They buy cashmere world wide, dehair it and sell it on the world market. The process involves passing the fibre through an air tunnel. The fine down rises up and the coarse guard hair falls downwards. Temperature and humidity have to be strictly monitored for a good result.

There are a few patented dehairers becoming available in the United States recently, but their product varies in quality. It is very easy to damage this fine fibre. Progress on designing dehairers is being made from sheer necessity, as Forte' will only accept bales of 500 lbs. for dehairing, obviously not a viable alternative for the small herd producer and cashmere will deteriorate if it is kept over a long period of time in the raw state, so growers are encouraged to ship their fleeces yearly.

PURCHASING & STORING CASHMERE FIBRE

Purchasing cashmere for spinning is an investment involving not only your money but your time, so here are some tips to remember.

The staple length should be at least 1½ to 2" in length and have very little or no lustre. Good cashmere has crimp which gives the fibre elasticity and "memory", which will allow the yarn to hold its twist and affect the drape of your finished garment. Fine cashmere will feel extremely soft to the touch, but not "silky" or sticky and there should be no debris or dandruff visible. Cashmere however has little strength and the fibres are easily damaged by commercial processing or over-zealous handcarding.

Look and feel for chemical or mechanical damage such as small nubs in the fibre. Be suspicious if the fibre is inexpensive, you may be looking at the waste after processing!

Buy enough fibre to finish your project, the overall fineness, colour and shade may vary between batches that are dehaired at different times.

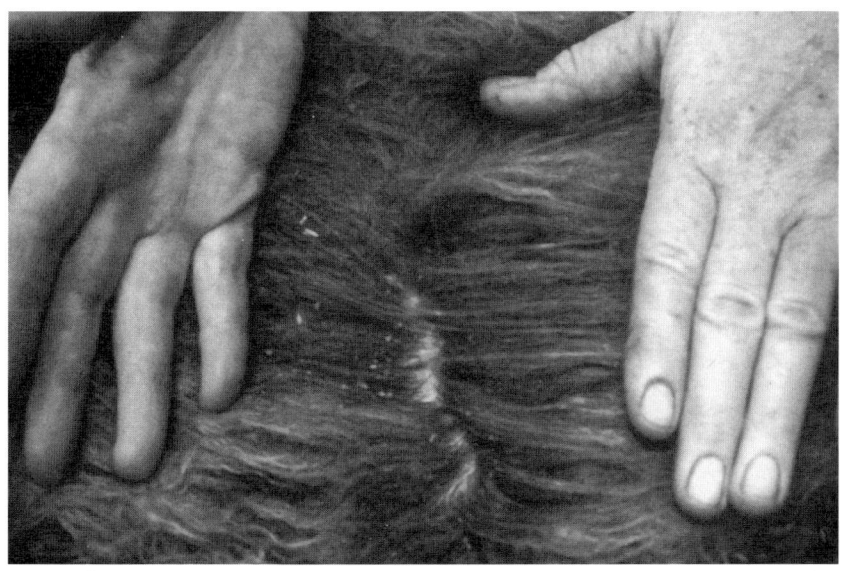

A Dense Cashmere Fleece

Storage:

Store your fibre in a rigid box, preferably of cardboard, in a cool place in your home. Seal any open ends of the box with tape so that no moths may enter. If you store your fibre in zip lock plastic bags, make sure they are kept cool, cashmere can felt quickly when hot or compressed.

Be aware that moths LOVE cashmere fibres, the more expensive and finer the better. It is a good idea to use herbs such as Eucalyptus or Pennyroyal to deter moths. Place the dried herbs in a gauze bag and place in with the cashmere. Cedar scented mothballs are available commercially and smell nicer than the original mothballs.

Some spinners refrigerate fibre to prevent moth damage. It also helps reduce static when spinning in a dry environment. Beware! Moths may hate the freezer section, but moth eggs can hibernate over winter and re-emerge in the Spring.

SPINNING CASHMERE

Spinning cashmere can be an intimidating experience for the novice spinner. It is extremely fine, usually short and very expensive. A few facts I discovered in my research will help allay fears and enable the hand spinner to enjoy this truly luxurious fibre.

Fibre Preparation:

If this fibre is purchased ready to spin, it has already been dehaired and scoured in that process. It can be spun with no further preparation unless you wish to card this fibre into punis or rolags. To make punis, take a small amount of cashmere and card, with cotton carders, using the third of the face of the carder away from the handle. Roll the carded fibre over a small diameter dowel, 1/4" wide and as long as the carder. Roll it firmly a few times on the wooden side of the carder, this compacts it, making it easy to remove in one piece.

I found that when carding this fibre, it was extremely easy to break it. If you must card, do so gently, barely allowing the carders to touch when you bring them together.

Punis
Step 1. Carding
Step 2. Rolling on a dowle
Step 3. Ready to spin

If the cashmere is still in the fleece, the coarse guard hair can be removed by hand. This is relatively easy if the fleece was combed rather than shorn. The former leaves most of the guard hair on the animal if the combing was done during the shedding cycle. Shearing removes all the guard hair with the down, and the ratio may be as much as 50/50 so there is a lot of coarse hair that must be painstakingly plucked out by hand.

Page 15

Spinning:

It is important not to hold too much fibre in the hand, this can felt it. Loosen the tension off of the brake band, but leave enough on to allow the fibre to be pulled in slowly. A supported long draw gives the smoothest result. If unsure of your skills, start spinning in your usual way, gradually lengthening the draughting zone and supporting the fibre with your free hand.

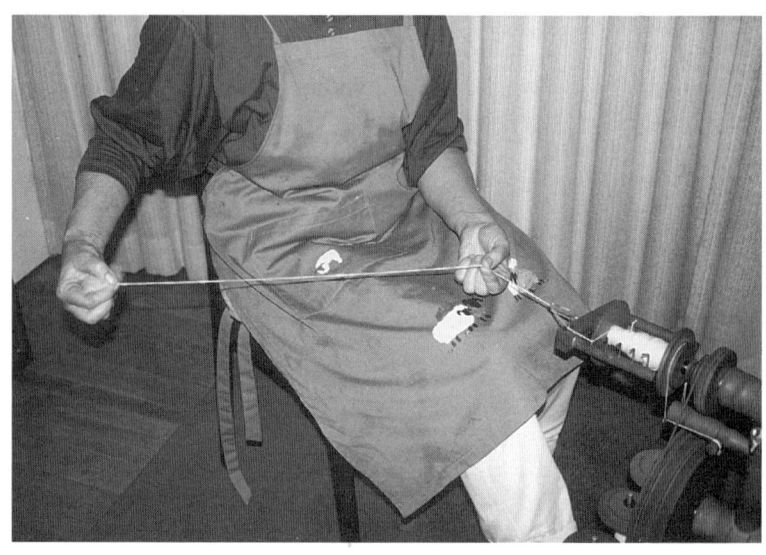

Supported long draw, pinching and attenuating

The spinning method I prefer is to start with a supported long draw. As soon as the draw is complete, still treadling, pinch the yarn at a few inches from the orifice of the wheel with your support hand. Gently attenuate the yarn in your spinning hand with two or three gentle pulls. This will remove any thick spots in your twist, producing an even yarn. Release the pinch and the twist will travel up the yarn. Allow this to draw in.

The ratio depends upon the wheel used, so sampling is necessary. Twist is needed, but not too much. Plying will remove some of the overtwist and make it softer to the hand. I found that if spun too finely, cashmere became hard to the hand.

Three ply produces a beautiful yarn that traps loft and knits up very nicely. When washed and fulled, it produces a delightful nap and the finished garment seems less likely to pill when worn.

Page 16

DYEING CASHMERE

Cashmere dyes beautifully, but care is needed to avoid felting the fibre if dyeing is done before spinning.

Method For Fibre:
i) Soak the cashmere fibre in warm soapy water in a container such as a metal sieve. If a small amount of liquid soap is used, there is no need to rinse before proceeding with the dyeing process. The container can then be lowered directly into the dye bath without the fibre being handled.

ii) Make sure that there is plenty of room for the fibre to float freely under the surface of the water. Too much fibre will cause an uneven result and hasten felting. If the fibre floats to the surface, push it down gently. You may have to place a wooden spoon or a tinfoil plate on top to keep it down. Avoid stirring more than necessary.

iii) After the dyeing process is completed, allow the fibre to stand in the water until it is cool enough to remove. This avoids shocking the fibre.

iv) A rinse in water of the same temperature or warmer, is advisable and adding a creme rinse conditioner will lessen static and protect the fibres.

v) Screen dry in a warm, airy place, avoiding the full sun.

Dyeing the Spun Yarn and Garments:

Dyeing the yarn or finished garment is safer, there is less chance of felting, but it is risky if you are a novice dyer. If the dyeing instruction are followed, the dye should be evenly distributed. Follow the same directions as described above. Make sure the skeins or garments are well scoured, skeins loosely tied and not overcrowded in the pot. Air dry the skeins without blocking to retain elasticity and softness.

BLENDING WITH CASHMERE

Cashmere is an exotic fibre and an expensive one. Prices in 1994 average $12 per ounce. Blending this fibre with a less expensive one is one of the best ways to make the most of cashmere. There are problems with some fibres as well as with some carding methods. Be sure to use a top quality fibre to blend with cashmere. There is no point wasting good cashmere when it is so costly.

CASHMERE and SILK:

Even though I blended this sample 50/50 the silk has taken over and minimized the effect of the cashmere. Because of the difference in these fibres, they had to be carded very well. Silk is a very strong fibre and is straight and slippery. The cashmere, however, is fine and has considerable crimp and elasticity. It broke easily when carded several times. When washed and fulled, the sample did not raise up a nice nap, but had a delightful lustre and a soft hand. Silk is a strong fibre and wears really well. It will prolong the longevity of your finished garment.

This blend takes up dye beautifully, but only if a homogenous blend, as the silk grabs the dye first. If you want a variegated effect, do not card the fibres quite so well. The silkier sections of your yarn will be more intense in colour and have more lustre.

CASHMERE and MERINO

These fibres I blended with a ratio of cashmere 1/3, Merino 2/3 at first. They had to be blended well because the Merino has far more crimp and elasticity than the cashmere, but each had an enhancing effect upon the other. The sample has the loft and elasticity of Merino, with the nap and handle of the cashmere.

CASHMERE and LAMBSWOOL

This 50/50 blend was easier to prepare than the Merino/cashmere blend because the lambswool had less crimp and elasticity. The result is a finer, more delicate yarn, with less loft than the Merino blend, but a softer handle. An inexpensive fibre, probably the best buy.

CASHHMERE and ANGORA

These fibres were blended 50\50 and carded together well because of the similarities. Both are very soft, semi-matte and with a tendency to felt easily. The blended sample was soft with a delightful nap. This is an excellent blend, although not the most economical, because of the price of Angora, which at the time of writing is $6.00 per ounce. The handle is the most luxurious of all the blends, each fibre enhancing the effects of the other. Really easy to spin and ply. Washing and dyeing would have to be done carefully. These two fibres react the same to shock, felting easily if handled when wet.

CONCLUSIONS:

If cashmere is blended with another fibre at less than a 50\50 ratio, the benefits of cashmere are diminished. The softness and nap are reduced. The higher the percentage of cashmere the easier the spinning. It is hard to justify spending money on good cashmere if it does not show up in the finished yarn. I recommend sampling before committing to a blend with this luxurious fibre.

Cashmere goats will climb anything!

WEAVING WITH CASHMERE

Weaving with cashmere is less expensive than knitting as less yardage is needed, and a great time saver if a commercial warp is used. Woven fabric is light and airy and a more traditional way to use a fibre that is so suited for the lace patterns that are available to the weaver.

I tested several of the blends of cashmere and other fibres that proved suitable for weaving. The ones I chose to use were the blends that kept their nap and loft when blended. Those that were dominated by their blends and lost those qualities were not deemed suitable.

The warp for my samples was a fine two ply pure cashmere warp from Hunt Valley Cashmere, Maryland. Traditionally, cashmere that falls in the 14-16 micron range is best suited for knitting and over that fine range is deemed suitable for weaving.

Hunt Valley Cashmere purchases fibre from China. The micron diameter is in the 14-16 range and the weight is 3,200 yards per pound. The harsh conditions in Mongolia, combined with scare food supplies in winter seem to contribute to the fineness of the cashmere. The yarn is purchased in pre-washed skeins so that only the finished article needs washing and fulling.

Of all the weft samples, the one with the best handle was the 100% cashmere. It fulled beautifully and was the lightest and softest next to the skin.

The Angora and cashmere blend was also very nice, but it had almost too much nap and might be too prickly to wear next to the skin. The lambswool and Merino blends were also good, but neither had the nap or the handle of the pure cashmere sample.

With all the other samples, I felt that with the work involved, the use of blends was not particularly economical. The 100% cashmere sample was worth the extra money involved for the fibre.

All the samples were washed in hot soapy water, using Ivory Liquid Soap, spun dry and fulled in the drier on the fluff cycle for a few minutes. The overall shrinkage was between 10-12% in the finished article. It was then pressed lightly with a damp cloth and fluffed again in the drier to raise the nap.

Some creme hair rinse or wool wash will protect the cashmere and help to act as a moth repellant. The more this fabric is handled the softer it will become.

The cashmere shawl I wove was a project that I longed to complete. I had participated in two "Cashmere to Shawl" events and was amazed at the softness of handspun yarn woven into a lace pattern. Each time the shawl was auctioned off I was outbidden, but now I finally have a family heirloom of my own.

My cashmere shawl

A CASHMERE SHAWL

Weave Structure:	Swedish lace weave.
Reed:	Number 8
Sett:	8 Sley 1-1-1
Number of ends:	218
Width:	27"
Length:	60"
Warp:	100% cashmere 2 ply. Hunt Valley Cashmere
Weft:	Handspun 2 ply yarn, from fibre purchased from Cashmere America.
Spinning:	I used a Peacock wheel, ratio 10:1. Spun Z using a supported long draw technique. Plied S and washed in hot water to set the twist.
Finished Width:	22"
Finished Length:	55" plus 10" fringe.
Pattern:	From A Handweaver's Pattern Book, Traditional Lace Unit # 1 by Marguerite Porter Davidson.
Finishing:	Washed in washing machine on delicate cycle with liquid Woolwash for 3 minutes. Spun to remove excess water and dried flat. Fluffed in drier for 10 minutes on delicate to raise nap.
Loom:	4 Harness Leclerc Inovation. Direct tie up.

I have washed this shawl several times now, and each washing raises the nap and makes it softer. Cashmere really improves with washing.

KNITTING WITH CASHMERE

Knitting with this exotic fibre is a very pleasant task. It is very soft and light weight but there are some points to think about before you start knitting. You have invested money in this project, so plan ahead.

If your hands are rough from working outside, use a non sticky hand cream. If your hand cream is too greasy you will have trouble holding on to metal needles and the stitches will slip off.

Sample, sample, sample. Before you start in earnest check needle gauge by making a swatch at least 4" square. Wash it well after knitting and measure the before and after size to ascertain shrinkage. Ribbing seems to stretch after washing, so sample the ribbing and if you like a snug rib change needle size, reduce the number of stitches and knit a twisted rib.

Cashmere is one of the warmest fibres, so a lacy pattern will produce a lighter, cooler garment and your yarn will go further. The initial shrinkage after knitting is about ten percent, but subsequent washing does cause some stretching if you are not careful. Here are a few methods I found helpful to retain the size and shape of my garments.

Washing in a machine raises the nap of the fabric beautifully but can stretch the garment. Using a light, open gauze bag of some kind, or arranging the garment lengthwise around in the washing machine limits the stretch. Wash on the delicate cycle for a few minutes, then rinse using a creme rinse if you used a soap. Stretch the garment back to the original shape and dry it flat.

Finish the drying process in the drier for a few minutes on the delicate cycle to raise the nap and restore the garment to its original condition. You may need to block it after drying, while it is still warm. The hot cycle on the drier will shrink your finished product.

Store the garment only when it is thoroughly dried, or it will felt if it gets agitated or hot. Fold it carefully, it does wrinkle, but a light pressing or steaming will soon restore it. Moths love expensive fibres, so when storing for a long time, a cedar chest or a closed container with moth repellents are good ideas.

Frequent washings will not damage cashmere as long as you use a gentle detergent and rinse. You will have a family heirloom if you look after it carefully.

Page 23

CASHMERE SCARF

Designed for Sandy Pines Farm by Lucy Neatby ©1996

MATERIALS: 1¼ ounces cashmere. Pair of 4mm needles.

ABBREVIATIONS:

Turn
-Turn the knitting around and work in the opposite direction, although unworked stitches remain on the left hand needle at this point.

K2t
-Knit 2 sts together, this produces a one stitch, right slanting decrease.

ssk
-Slip, slip, knit. Slip the next two stitches, knitwise,one at a time,to the right hand needle. Insert the left hand needle into both stitches and knit them together. This produces a one stitch, left slanting decrease.

sl1, k2t,psso
-Slip one stitch knitwise from left to right needle, K2tog, pass the slipped stitch over the st just worked. This is a two stitch decrease.

O
-Yarn over needle, forming a new stitch.

inc
-Increase one stitch by knitting into the stitch below the one that has just been worked.

K3t
-Knit three stitches together.

Use lightweight needles for easier working.

Make triangle strip.
With 4 mm needles, loop cast on 25 stitches. Knit one row.
#Knit 2 sts, turn. (at this point there will be 23 sts remaining unworked.)
** K2
K2sts + 1st from the remaining 23,turn.   K3.
K3sts + 1st from those remaining, turn.   K4.
K4sts + 1st from those remaining, turn.   K5.
K5sts + 1st from those remaining, turn.   K6.
K6sts + 1st from those remaining, turn.   K7.

Next Row Cast off 6 sts, (This leaves one stitch on the right hand needle.) Knit one stitch from those remaining. (2sts on RH needle). Turn.**
Repeat from ** to ** 3 times more, ending with one st remaining after casting off for the fourth triangle.
Loop cast on 7 more stitches, 8 in total.
Knit these 8 stitches, and knit up a further 33 across the bases of the four triangles. (8 for each triangle + one in the middle), end by loop casting on a further 7 sts. (48sts)

row 1.   wrong side. k7, k2t, o2, k3, o, k2t, k2, p16, k4, o, k2t, k1, o2, k2t, k7
row 2.   right side. k9, p1, k3, o, k2t, k2,(o, ssk,k4, k2t)x2, o, k4, o, k2t, k2, p1, k8.
row 3.   k13. o, k2t, k2, p15, k4, o, k2t, k11.
row 4.   k13, o, k2t, k2, o, ssk, k3, k2t, o, k1, o, ssk, k3, k2t, o, k4, o, k2t, k11.
row 5.   k6, (k2t,o2)x2, k3, o, k2t, k2, p15, k4, o, k2t, k1, (o2,k2t)x2, k6.
row 6.   k8, p1, k2, p1, k3, o, k2t, k2, o, ssk, k2, k2t, o, k3, o, ssk, k2, k2t, o, k4, o, k2t, (k2, p1)x2, k7.
row 7.   k15, o, k2t, k2, p15, k4, o, k2t, k13.
row 8.   k15, o, k2t, k2, o, ssk, k1, k2t, o, k1, o, (sl1,k2t,psso), o, k1, o, ssk, k1, k2t, o, k4, o, k2t, k13.
row 9.   k6, (k2t, o2)x3, k3, o, k2t, k2, p15, k4, o, k2t, k1, (o2, k2t)x3, k6.
row 10. k8, p1, (k2, p1)x2, k3, o, k2t, k2, o, ssk, k2t, o, k4, inc 1, k3, o, ssk, k2t, o, k4, o, k2t,(k2,p1)x3, k7.
row 11. cast off 6 (leaves 1st on right hand needle), k11, o, k2t, k2, p16, k4, o, k2t, k16.
row 12. cast off 6 (leaves 1st on right hand needle), k11, o, k2t, k2, o, (sl1, k2t, psso), o, k10, o, k3t, o, k4, o, k2t, k10.

Repeat these twelve rows until the scarf is the desired length.
One ounce of cashmere will require 15 repeats, ending with a washed, scarf of 30 " in length. Finish with a twelfth row. 48 stitches. Leave stitches on needle.

Final Triangles

Knit the first 7 sts, turn. Leave the remaining 41 sts on the needle.

Knit these 7 sts, 9 times more, cast off 7, break off yarn. Rejoin the yarn to the remaining stitches.

k3, (k1,k2t)x9, k4, turn,(this leaves 7 sts unworked)

Across the 25 stitches that you have just worked, repeat the initial triangle strip beginning at #, ending with cast off 7 after the fourth triangle. Break off yarn.

Rejoin yarn to the final 7 sts. Knit these 7 sts, 10 times, cast off 7, break off yarn.

Darn in ends.

WASHING INSTRUCTIONS.

I use Woolwash/Euclan/Lanocreme, one capful in a washing machine of warm water. Allow to agitate for three minutes, then spin dry. There is no need to rinse with this product. If you use a detergent, make sure it is a liquid one, then rinse well and spin again. Gently stretch scarf into the original shape and line dry. Finish in the drier for a few minutes, to fluff it up nicely.

The scarf will become softer with each washing.

Spring pasture

Page 26

PATTI'S CASHMERE BONNET AND BOOTIES

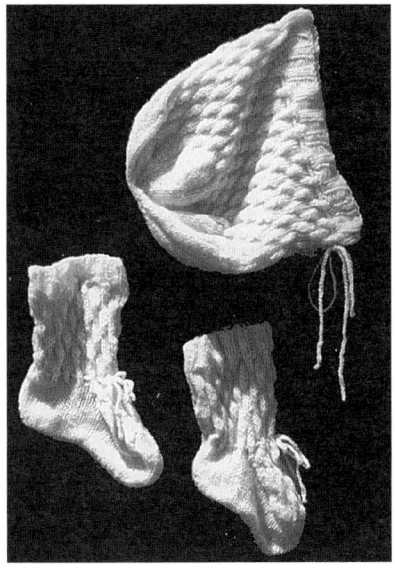

Designed for Sandy Pines Farm by Patti Walker ©1996

MATERIALS: 1¼ ounces cashmere. Pair of 3¼ and 3¾ mm needles.

BONNET:
With larger needles cast on 94 sts. Change to smaller needles and work 10 rows in k2p2 rib, inc. 44 sts. in last row (138). Ribbon Row: k1, yo k2 tog.to end. Purl one row.

PATTERN:
row 1. k1, *k3, sl 3 purlwise with yarn behind work. Repeat from * to last five stitches. k5.
row 2. p2, * p3, sl 3 purlwise with yarn in front of work. Repeat from * to last four stitches. p4.
row 3. as row 1.
row 4. as row 2.
row 5. k1*, k3 yarn forward and over needle to make a stitch, sl 2 stitches as if to work 2 tog. k1. pass 2 slipped stitches over. Yarn over needle. Repeat from * to last five stitches. k5.
row 6. purl.
row 7. kl, *sl 3 purlwise with yarn behind work, k3. Repeat from * to last five stitches. sl 3 purlwise, k2.
row 8. p2*, sl 3 purlwise with yarn in front of work, p3. Repeat from * to last four stitches. sl 3 purlwise, p1.
row 9. as row 7.

row 10. as row 8.

row 11. k1* yarn forward and over needle to make a stitch, slip 2 stitches as if to work 2 tog., k1, pass slipped stitches over. yarn forward and over needle to make a stitch. k3. repeat from * to last two stitches. k2.

row 12. purl.

Pattern repeat 3 more times.

Crown: k8, k2 tog. to end. alt rows purl.

k7, k2 tog. to end.

Continue to decrease right down to k0 k2 tog.,purl one row then k2 tog. break yarn and draw end through 7 sts. on needle. sew seam from crown to three inches from cast on edge.

BOOTIES:

With larger needles cast on 36 sts. Change to smaller needles and knit 8 rows in double rib.(k2, p2), increasing 6 sts. in last row.

Repeat pattern twice.

Ribbon row: k1 Yarn over needle to make stitch, k2 tog. Repeat to end.

Toe: P 12, pattern on next 18 stitches for the toe flap (start with row 2.P3, slip three sts purlwise).

Complete two patterns on toe flap.

Slip 18 toe stitches onto needle with 12 unpurled stitches; break wool.

Join wool after first 12 purled stitches; pick up purlwise 12 stitches along side of toe; purl across 18 toe stitches; pick up and knit 12 stitches along other side of toe; purl across remaining twelve stitches. (66 stitches).

Knit 6 rows stocking stitch.

k2 tog, k62, k2 tog.

purl

k2 tog, k60, k2 tog.

purl

k2 tog, k58, k2 tog.

purl

cast off.

Sew seams and add ribbon for ties.

Follow washing instructions for sweater.

TOQUE AND BOOTIES FOR A NEWBORN

Designed for Sandy Pines Farm by Sue Meech ©1996

MATERIALS: 1 ounce of cashmere. Pair or 3½ and 4 mm needles.

Using 3.5 mm needles cast on 88 stitches and work in double rib (K2P2) for 2 inches.

Change to size 4 needles.

Pattern:

row 1. knit

row 2. purl

row 3. knit

row 4. * p1, yarn over needle and around to front and p2 together* repeat from * to * to last stitch, p1.

row 5. knit

row 6. purl

row 7. knit

row 8. p2, *yarn over needle and around to front and p2 together, p1* repeat from * to * to last two stitches, yarn over needle and around to front, p2 together. Continue pattern until 5" has been worked from cast on edge.

crown:

k1(k2 tog, k5)repeat to the end.

alternate rows purl.

3rd row:k1(k2 tog. k4) repeat to end.

Keep decreasing in this manner until 13th row. k2 tog. to end.

Break wool and run end through remaining stitches.

Sew seam and finish with Pom pom.

BOOTIES:

Using no 4.needles cast on 33 stitches
Pattern 12 rows.

row 13. knit

row 14. purl

row 15. for ribbon.k2,(yarn forward, k 2 tog. k1) repeat to end.

row 16. purl

row 17. instep: k 22 turn. p 11 turn. Working on these 11 sts. work 12 rows in stocking stitch, break yarn. With right side facing join yarn to instep at the end of the first 11 stitches and pick up k9 along right side, k11 across and k9 along left side, k remaining 11 stitches. (51). Stocking stitch 7 rows.

foot: k1, k 2 tog., k17, k2 tog through back loop, k7, k2 tog.,k17,k2 tog. through back of loop, k1.

2nd row: purl.

3rd row: k1, k2 tog., k16, k2 tog. through back of loop, k5, k2 tog.k16, k2 tog. through back of loop, k1.

4th row: purl. cast off. sew seams and add ribbon at ankle.

Follow washing instructions for sweater.

CASHMERE POLO SWEATER

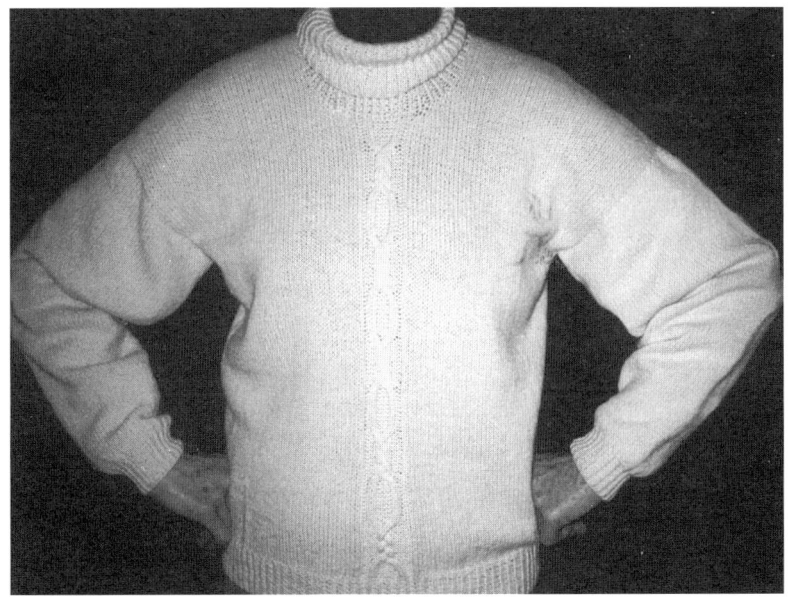

Designed for Sandy Pines Farm by Patti Walker ©1996

MATERIAL: SIZE (Sm) (Md) (Lg)
16 OZ. 4 ply cashmere yarn for Large
1 pr. 3 mm needles 1 pr. 4 mm needles
For snug ribbing use twisted rib throughout the garment, by knitting into the back of the knit stitches.

BACK:
With 3 mm needles cast on (85)(97)(107) stitches. Rib 20 rows increasing (27)(27)(29) stitches on last rib row. Total stitches (112)(124)(136). With 4 mm. needles, knit to desired length. Cast off leaving centre (28)(32)(36) stitches on a needle for neck.

FRONT:
Work rib as for back but increase (25)(25)(27) on last rib row. Total stitches (116)(128)(140). Place cable in centre after (56)(57)(63) stitches.

Page 31

Work cable Pattern:

row 1.   p2,k2,p6,k2,p2
row 2.   k2,p2,k6,p2,k2

Repeat these two rows twice.

row 7.   p2, slip next 2 stitches onto cable needle, hold at front. p2, k2, then k2 from cable needle. slip 2 stitches onto cable needle, leave at back, k2, then p2 from cable needle, p2.
row 8.   p4, k6, p4
row 9.   p4, k2, slip next two stitches onto cable needle, hold at back of work, k2, k2 from cable needle, p4
row 10.   as row 8
row 11.   p4,slip next two stitches onto cable needle and hold at front, k2, k2 from cable needle, k2 p4.
row 12.   as row 8
row 13.   as row 9
row 14.   as row 8
row 15.   as row 11
row 16.   as row 8
row 17.   as row 9
row 18.   as row 8
row 19.   p2, slip next 4 stitches onto cable needle, hold at back, k2, then p4 from cable needle. slip next two stitches onto cable needle, hold at front, p2, k2 from cable needle, p2.
row 20.   as row 2
row 21.   as row 1
row 22.   as row 2
row 23.   as row 1
row 24.   as row 2

Continue in cable pattern for desired length.

Next row Knit (52)(53)(59). Knit 2 together for neck edge, turn.

Decrease one stitch at neck edge on next 3 rows, then alternate rows (3)(5)(7) times.

Continue even for 24 rows.

Cast off. Slip next 18 stitches onto stitch holder for front. Knit 2 together(neck edge). Work to correspond to other side, reversing all shapings.

Page 32

SLEEVES:

With 3 mm needles cast on(43)(43)(45) stitches. Rib 18 rows, Increase (21)(25)(27) stitches over the last row. Total stitches (64)(68)(72). Change to 4 mm needles. Increase one stitch on either end of 5th then every 4th row 12 times, then every 6th row to (106)(110)(114) stitches total. Work straight to desired length from ribbing. Cast off.

COLLAR:

Sew right shoulder seam. With right side of work facing and 4 mm needles, pick up and knit 17 stitches down left front neck edge.

Knit 18 stitches from front stitch holder. Pick up and knit 17 stitches up right front neck edge. Knit across (28)(32)(36) stitches from back stitch holder- Total stitches (80)(84)(88).

Work 7 inches in rib. Cast off in rib.

Join left shoulder seam and neck. Mark for sleeves (8)(8.5)(9) inches from shoulder centre down back and front. Sew sleeves in place. Sew sleeve and side seams.

WASHING GARMENT:

I use Woolwash\Euclan, which requires no rinsing. Soak 15 minutes in washing machine, then agitate on delicate cycle for four minutes. Spin out water, stretch to original shape and dry flat.

Fluff in drier on delicate cycle for two minutes when almost dry.

Store in a dry, cool area of your closet. If cashmere gets hot and wet it may felt. Moths love cashmere, but the Eucalyptus in the Woolwash\Euclan will help repel them.

If you use a detergent, make sure it is a gentle liquid one. Dish washer liquid is excellent. Rinse well and dry as above. You may use a small amount of hair conditioner in the rinse to maintain the fibre in optimum condition.

CLASSIC CABLED CASHMERE

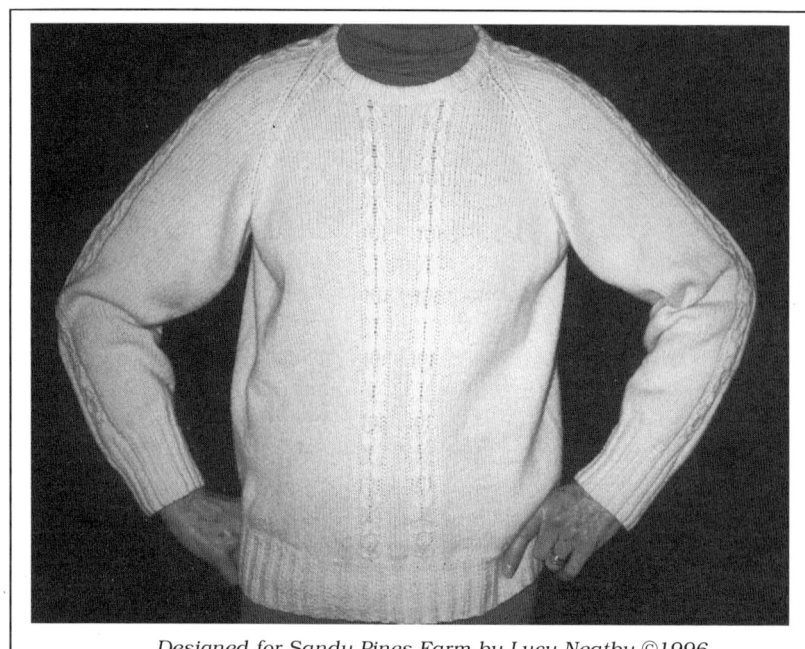

Designed for Sandy Pines Farm by Lucy Neatby ©1996

MATERIAL: SIZE Sm - 43" (Md 45") (Lg 47")
16 OZ. 4 ply cashmere yarn for Large

NEEDLES: 1 pr. 3 mm needles, 1 pr. 4 mm needles
plus a 3mm circular needle.
Substitute sizes to meet given gauge.

GAUGE: With 4mm needles and stocking stitch, 21 sts and
30 rows = 4" square

ABBREVIATIONS

kb   - Knit into the back of the stitch, this twists the
stitch below and tightens up the ribbings.

pb   - Purl into the back of the stitch, this twists the
stitch below and tightens up the ribbing, (neck
only).

k2t   - Knit 2 sts together, this produces a one stitch,
right slanting decrease.

ssk   - Slip, slip, knit. Slip the next two sts, knitwise,

	one at a time, to the righthand needle, insert the lefthand needle into both sts and knit them together. This produces a one stitch, left slanting decrease.
ssp	- Slip, slip, purl. Slip the next two sts from the left to right needle in order, knitwise, place the tip of the left hand needle below and into the first stitch to be slipped, then into the second slipped stitch and return them to the lefthand needle, (this reverses their order), p2t. This produces a 1st left slanting decrease when worked on a WS row.
LSI	- Left slanting increase, increase one stitch by knitting into the stitch below the one that has just been worked.
RSI	- Right slanting increase, increase one stitch by knitting into the stitch below the one that is next on the left hand needle.
c2b	- Place next 2 sts on a cable needle at the back of the work, knit the next st, knit the 2sts from the cable needle. (A 3 stitch cable)
c1f	- Place next st on a cable needle at the front of the work, knit the next 2sts, knit the stitch from the cable needle. (A 3 stitch cable)
c2bp	- Place next 2 sts on a cable needle at the back of the work, knit the next st, purl the 2sts from the cable needle. (A 3 stitch cable)
c1fp	- Place next st on a cable needle at the front of the work, purl the next 2sts, knit the stitch from the cable needle. (A 3 stitch cable)
RS	- Right Side
WS	- Wrong Side

NOTES

All the knit stitches in the rib are worked into the back of the stitch in order to give extra firmness, (there is a slight variation for the neckband, see specific instructions). Resist the temptation to be extra firm with (or to slip) the outermost stitch on the raglan deceases, if they are too firm they will distort the line of the raglan, due to the relative inelasticity of cashmere. This column of stitches may look a little raggy, but they disappear inside the garment once it is mattress stitched together. To avoid confusion, highlight the details of the particular size you are working. There is no cable pattern up the back of the sweater. With the large areas of stocking stitch avoid attempting to join new yarns in the middle of a row. To check if you have sufficient yarn for a whole row, allow a yarn length of about 4 times the width of the knitting, to safely complete the whole row without running out. To adjust body length, either alter the ribbing length or omit 1 pattern rpt (approx 2.5") in the main body section, and adjust the number of rows in the back by 16 rows.

BACK

Length from shoulder: 23" (24", 25")

Ribbing	With smaller (3mm) needles cast on 102 (106, 110) sts.
Row 1.	RS	Kb 2, (p2, kb 2) to end of row.
Row 2.	WS	P2, (kb 2, p2) to end of row.

Repeat these two rows until Row 29 is completed.

Row 30.
(Small&Large)   In the rib pattern, inc 5 (7) sts evenly across the first 40 (44) sts, (p2, kb2) x 2, p2, inc 1st in each of next two sts, (p2, kb2) x 2, p2, inc 5(7) sts evenly across the last 40 (44) sts. 114 (126) sts.

Row 30.
(Medium)   In the rib pattern, inc 6 sts evenly across the first 42sts, (kb2, p2) x 2, kb2, inc 1st in each of next two sts, (kb2, p2) x 2, kb2, inc 6 sts evenly across the last 42 sts. (120) sts.

Change to larger (4mm) needle and work in stocking stitch beginning with a knit row, for 68 (64, 70) rows.

*Work 8 (20, 18) more rows of stocking stitch before beginning shapings.

Cast off 4 (5, 5) sts at the beginning of the next two rows. Decrease 1st at the beginning and end of the next 16 (18, 20) rows, as follows:-

| RS | K2, ssk, knit to last four sts, k2t, k2. |
| WS | P2, p2t, purl to last four sts, ssp, p2. |

Dec 1st at each end of every RS row as previously given and purl the WS rows, until the correct number of stitches is reached, 32 (32, 34)
Work a final purl row. *
Slip the stitches onto a thread or stitch holder.

FRONT

Work as given for Back until ribbing Row 30 is completed.

Change to larger (4mm) needles, work the following two rows,
2 (0, 3) times.

RS   Knit 45 (48, 51) sts, p2, k6, p2, k4, p2, k6, p2, knit
            remaining 45 (48, 51) sts.
WS   Purl 45 (48, 51) sts, k2, p6, k2, p4, k2, p6, k2, purl
            remaining 45 (48, 51) sts.

All sizes, work the 16 row cable pattern rpt, four times.

Row 1. RS   Knit 45 (48, 51) sts, p2, k6, p2, k4, p2, k6, p2,
            knit remaining 45 (48, 51) sts.
Row 2. WS   Purl 45 (48, 51) sts, k2, p6, k2, p4, k2, p6, k2,
            purl remaining 45 (48, 51) sts.
Row 3.   Knit 45 (48, 51) sts, p2, c2b, c1f, p2, k4, p2, c2b,
            c1f, p2, knit remaining 45 (48, 51) sts.
Row 4.   As Row 2.
Row 5.   As Row 1.
Row 6.   As Row 2.
Row 7.   Knit 45 (48, 51) sts, p2, c2bp, c1fp, p2, k4, p2,
            c2bp, c1fp, p2, knit remaining 45(48, 51) sts.
Row 8.   Purl 45 (48, 51) sts, k2, p1, k4, p1, k2, p4, k2, p1,
            k4, p1, k2, purl remaining 45 (48, 51) sts.
Row 9.   Knit 45 (48, 51) sts, p2, k1, p4, k1, p2, k4, p2, k1,
            p4, k1, p2, knit remaining 45 (48, 51) sts.
Row 10.   As Row 8.
Row 11.   Knit 45 (48, 51) sts, p2, c1f, c2b, p2, k4, p2, c1f,
            c2b, p2, knit remaining 45 (48, 51) sts.
Row 12.   As Row 2
Row 13.   As Row 1.
Row 14.   As Row 2.
Row 15.   As Row 11.
Row 16.   As Row 2.

Work from * to *, as for back, continuing the cable, and shaping
the neck as follows.

Neck Shapings

When 52 (52, 54) sts remain, commence neck shapings on the
next RS row. K2, ssk, k 16 (16, 17), turn the work around.
WS Row   Cast off 4 (loosely), purl to end of row.

RS Dec Row K2, ssk, knit to 3sts before the end, k2t, k1.
WS Dec Row P1, p2t, purl to end,

Work RS and WS decrease rows alternately until 5 (5,6) sts have
been decreased by this method. Continue to decrease on the
raglan edge only, as usual until 3 sts remain. After this point,

on RS rows, work the dec at the neck edge, until only one stitch remains.

Slip the middle 12 sts onto a stitch holder or thread of yarn, rejoin the yarn to remaining stitches, work as usual to the end of the row. Continue, reversing the shapings given for the left side of neck, using ssk RS and ssp WS decs at the neck edge.

SLEEVES - Length from neck 24.5" (25", 25.5") where three numbers are shown they relate to S (M, L) respectively. If any length adjustment is desired, shorten or lengthen the cuff accordingly.

With smaller (3mm) needles cast on 66 (70, 70) sts.
Row 1.   RS Kb 2, (p2, kb 2) to end of row.
Row 2,.   WS P2, (kb 2, p2) to end of row.
Repeat these two rows until Row 29 (33, 35) is completed.

Inc Row (small)	In the rib pattern, inc 3 sts evenly across the first 28 sts, (p2, kb2) x 2, p2, inc 3 sts evenly across the last 28 sts. Total 72 sts.

Inc Row (med.&large)	In the rib pattern, inc (3,5) sts evenly across the first (30,30) sts, (kb2, p2) x 2, kb2, inc (3,5) sts evenly across the last (30,30) sts. (76,80) sts.

Change to larger (4mm) needles. Check that the reverse stocking stitch stripes on either side of the cable panel are in the correct position, but do not start the cable pattern until the third (fifth, seventh) row of the sleeve.

SMALL
Row 1. RS   K31, p2, k6, p2, k31 (72sts).
Row 2. WS   P31, k2, p6, k2, p31.
Row 3.   As Row 1 - this is Cable Row 1 also.
Row 4.   As Row 2.
Row 5.   K2, RSI, k29, Cable Row 3, k29, LSI, k2.

Continue sleeve incs every following 10th row, 8 times more, 90sts total. Continue in cable pattern up the sleeve.
Row 91, Commence raglan shapings.

MEDIUM
Row 1 RS   K33, p2, k6, p2, k33. (76sts).
Row 2 WS   P33, k2, p6, k2, p33.
Row 3.   As Row 1.
Row 4.   As Row 2.
Row 5.   K2, RSI, k31, Cable Row 1, k31, LSI, k2.

Continue sleeve incs every folowing 10th row, 8 times more, 94sts total. Continue in cable pattern up the sleeve.
Row 91, Commence raglan shapings.

LARGE
Row 1 RS   K35, p2, k6, p2, k35. (80sts).
Row 2 WS   P35, k2, p6, k2, p35.
Row 3.   As Row 1.
Row 4.   As Row 2.
Row 5.   K2, RSI, knit to last 2 sts, LSI, k2.
Row 6.   P36, k2, p6, k2, p36.
Row 7.   K36, Cable Row 1, k36.

Continue sleeve incs every folowing 10th row, 8 times more, 98sts total. Continue in cable pattern up the sleeve.
Row 91, Commence raglan shapings.

CABLE PATTERN - work on the central 10 sts of the sleeve, commencing on the third (fifth, seventh) row of the sleeve.

Cable Row 1. RS   P2, k6, p2.
Cable Row 2. WS   K2, p6, k2.
Cable Row 3.   P2, c2b, c1f, p2.
Cable Row 4.   As Cable Row 2.
Cable Row 5.   As Cable Row 1.
Cable Row 6.   As Cable Row 2.
Cable Row 7.   P2, c2bp, c1fp, p2.
Cable Row 8.   K2, p1, k4, p1, k2.
Cable Row 9.   P2, k1, p4, k1, p2.
Cable Row 10.   As Row 8.
Cable Row 11.   P2, c1f, c2b, p2.
Cable Row 12.   As Cable Row 2
Cable Row 13.   As Cable Row 1.
Cable Row 14.   As Cable Row 2.
Cable Row 15.   As Cable Row 11.
Cable Row 16.   As Cable Row 2.

Raglan shapings. Maintain cable pattern throughout.

Cast off 4 (5, 5) sts at the beginning of the next two rows. Decrease 1st at the beginning and end of the next 14 (14, 16) rows, as follows:-

RS   K2, ssk, knit to last four sts, k2t, k2.
WS   P2, p2t, purl to last four sts, ssp, p2.

Dec 1st at each end of every RS row as previously given and purl the WS rows, until 12sts remain on the WS row.

Right sleeve top, work as follows :- K2, ssk, k3, casting off the stitches loosely as you go, (1st remains on RH needle, work to end of row as usual. Purl back, cast off loosely.
Left Sleeve top, Work a final RS row. On the following WS row, cast off loosely purlwise the first half of the stitches, purl to end. Turn and cast off remaining sts loosely, knitwise.

FINISHING
Block the four pieces of the garment by pinning into desired shape with rustless pins, lightly mist with cold water, pat into position, leave to dry naturally. Do not stretch the ribbings! Join the raglans together using mattress stitch.

NECKBAND
   With smaller (3mm) 40cm circular needle, right side of work facing, knit up 96 (96, 100) stitches as follows, starting at the left sleeve.
   Across the top of the LH sleeve, knit up 2sts in each raglan decrease and 2st in between them, (6sts).
21 (21, 23) sts down left front to the stitches on a holder, 12 sts from the holder, 21 (21, 23) sts across right front, 6st across RH sleeve (as LH sleeve) and 30 sts across the back of neck Large only - k2t in two places to achieve the right number of sts).
   When picking up the raw sts from the stitch holder across the back of the neck remember to secure the raw st on the inside of the mattress st seam. This can be done by putting the needle through the second stich on the holder and also the raw st on the inside and working them as one stitch.
   Place a yarn marker at the beginning/end point of the round, to remind you to change from knitting into the back of the knit sts to working into the back of the purl sts (alternate rounds). If the stitches are picked up as shown, the centre two sts of the cable panel will line up with either a p2 (sm) or k 2 (md,lg) in the neck and look attractive.

Round 1.   Kb2, p2, to end of round.
Round 2.   K2, pb2, to end of round.
Repeat these two rounds three times more.
Round 9.   Pb2, p2, to end of round. (Turning row)
Round 10. P2, kb2, to end of round.
Round 11. Pb2, k2, to end of round.
Repeat these two rounds three times more.

Either cast off very loosely and catch stitch to the inside of the neck, or (best way for maximum elasticity) graft the raw stitches to the inside of the neck. Ensure that the columns of knit and purl lie straight as you stitch/graft into place. An elastic thread may be inserted in the neck at any time, should a firmer edge be required.

Sew up side seams using mattress st, begin at the cuffs and lower edges of the garment and sew towards the under arm. When seaming is complete, darn in any ends.

BLOCKING
Lay garment out, pin into desired shape with rustless pins, lightly mist with cold water, pat into position, leave to dry naturally.

WASHING INSTRUCTIONS
By Machine - using Lanocreme \ Euclan \ Woolwash and warm water, agitate for 3 minutes and spin out water. If using a liquid detergent add a creme hair conditioner to the rinse water.
Reshape whilst still damp. Pay particular attention to ribbings, to allow them to regain their elasticity, scrunch them up well whilst drying. Allow the garment to dry flat on a towel until almost dry. Complete drying in a drier for 3 minutes to fluff up and soften the Cashmere. The sweater will become softer with each wash.
Store in a cool dry place, Cashmere will only felt if damp and overheated, such as in a plastic bag. Be warned, moths love fine fibres! Use a moth repellant when storing over the summer. Eucalyptus oil is great.

RAISING CASHMERE GOATS

Many spinners and fibre enthusiasts enjoy raising their own fibre animals. I began by raising my own sheep and Angora goats and started to plan raising cashmere goats several years ago. I knew very little about these animals and learned about them by trial and error.

Here are some things to consider before you make an investment.

CASHMERE GOATS

These goats have been feral for generations and because of evolution and a survival of the fittest, they are hardy and very smart. Here are some pointers.

FENCING:

You need good fencing, with narrow gauge , at least five feet in height and as close to the ground as you can get it. These agile goats can get under a gap of 2 inches if they wish, by pushing their noses under first. These goats are also good at getting their heads stuck in the fence and cannot pull back because of their horns. If all fails they will try to jump a fence to get to the greener pasture on the other side, or a good looking buck.

I recommend a five foot fence with a strand of barbed wire stretched above it at six feet. Be sure to check your fences in the Spring before turning the goats out on fresh pasture. Frost can cause posts to heave, leaving just enough room for a goat to squeeze under.

I know that some people have success with electric fencing, but it has not worked for me, the goats seem to know immediately the current is off, which seems to happen frequently as the grass grows and the summer pasture becomes dry.

HOUSING:

These goats are hardy but do need shelter from cold winds in the Northern areas. Shelter may vary according to the climate from none in the South to a barn in the North. In Southern States, little shelter is required, and the goats roam freely. In Canada, my goats are housed in a three sided structure, facing South. Cashmere down is at its maximum density during our coldest season and they do well even in the coldest winters. At kidding time, I provide an enclosed pen and a heat lamp if necessary, but in warmer climates the goats kid outside.

PURCHASING YOUR GOATS:

I encourage all prospective goat breeders to join their Regional Cashmere Association, (see Resources in the Appendix). You will be put in touch with a reputable breeder who will guide you through purchasing and be a contact for further advice from time to time.

Prices for quality animals has fallen to a reasonable $200 and up at the time of writing, so you can afford to buy the best possible animals for your breeding program. Remember that your buck will be providing genes for half of your herd, so spend time choosing a suitable animal.

Examine the fleece, or ask a knowledgable person to help you. Down tends to coarsen with the age of the goat, so while you would accept a down with medium micron diameter on an older buck, you should expect to see a finer down on a kid.

Look at overall shape and size. It is pointless to have a super fine fleece on an animal that is weak or has some major problem with conformation. If you do not have sufficient knowledge about goats, a Veterinary opinion would be a good idea. A reputable breeder will help you decide your priorities and goals when buying stock and will not be offended by a request for a Veterinarian check.

FEEDING:

Cashmere goats do well on marginal land and prefer weeds, low bushes and trees where they can browse, to grass pasture. In cold climates they need hay in the winter but not the high protein hay that some animals require.

To keep their rumen healthy, they need a high percentage of roughage and little grain. In areas where they are out grazing all year round they are not usually fed any supplementary grain.

They do need access to fresh water, but will eat snow if thirsty. I give my goats warm water when it is very cold and they drink it quickly.

All animals need minerals in their diet for healthy fibre production and some will require supplementary minerals depending upon on the area that you live in and the soil analysis. Many areas in Canada are Selenium deficient and the goats and kids can acquire White Muscle Disease if they are not supplemented at birth.

I supply mixed minerals free choice all year round and salt, free choice during the hottest months of the year.

FLEECE:
The down starts to grow in early summer and it continues to grow until mid-winter. At this point you have to decide what to do. In the Southern States shearing is done early in the year, but in Northern climates, you risk losing your animals to hypothermia if you have a severe cold spell after shearing.

Combing can be done when the fleece starts to shed. The timing of this shedding depends on the animal and the climate. I have some goats that can be combed in January, but some seem to keep their fleece on until May. These I usually shear to avoid a sudden shedding and loss of fibre from rubbing on fences. Combing can be done weekly over a period of two or three weeks, or all at once if the fleece combs off easily. Each animal has different traits regarding shedding.

When you have gathered your fibre, weigh and examine it for length , style and diameter, so that you can keep accurate records to identify your best animals for breeding. Store the fleece in a dry, cool place and preferably in sealed bags, as moths love fine fibres.

You have a few choices about dealing with your fibre. You can sell it, as it is, to a buyer. There a some private buyers that run small businesses and some can dehair their fibre. You can join a Co-op and send your fibre to a pool to be dehaired and have the choice of being paid cash, or a product such as down or yarn. Your third option is to find a business with a dehairer,that will dehair small orders of cashmere and return your own fibre . There are a few small companies that will do this, but the results seem very variable. Be careful about storing your fleece as it will deteriorate over time.

CULLING:

This means disposing of your goats that do not have good fibre traits, or show conformation faults. You will have to face the fact, sooner or later, that you cannot afford to keep all your goats, only the best ones. You also cannot sell breeding stock that is not of good quality. There is a market for chevon or goat meat. Explore the possibilities in your area.

You will enjoy cashmere goats and you will never be bored, but do not expect to get rich, especially when you first start in the business. Learn as much as you can, get together with other goat herders and you may eventually make raising cashmere profitable.

MARKETING

If you wish to succeed in business, you have to market your goods. Selling cashmere fibre, breeding stock and meat is no different, you have to let consumers know that you have a quality product for sale. Here are a few tips.

CASHMERE FIBRE:

There is very little or no market for your raw fleeces except to large wool buyers (See Resources) because of the problem of guard hairs. Time is too precious for most spinners to waste it picking out hairs. You will need to get dehaired fleece and try to offer a variety of colours.

Know your fibres. Spinners are very educated and know what they want. If you give them a quality product, you will have repeat customers.

You can learn about cashmere from your local groups and Newsletters, but if you learn to work with cashmere yourself, you will meet potential customers and learn at the same time. Most areas of North America have Spinning and Weavers Groups who would love to hear from you. Most will help you learn to spin, weave and dye cashmere. Good cashmere fibre and yarn are hard to find for their special projects, so take samples to the meetings.

Attend Fibre Festivals, there are several large, well know ones, such as The Maryland Sheep and Wool Festival, and FiberFest in Ohio (Used to be in Michigan), but there are lots of smaller local ones that spinners, knitters and weavers attend.

CASHMERE YARN:

There are more knitters than spinners so you should plan to have your fibre made into yarn or buy cashmere yarn wholesale and become a supplier.

There are several lovely natural colours and blends available and you may be able to do some custom dyeing for your customers.

Novice knitters like to have a pattern to follow for the yarn they have bought, (hopefully from you!) so experiment and design simple patterns for baby sets, scarves etc. Smaller projects sell much better than large ones, because of the price involved. Be aware of Copywrite laws and do not copy a pattern without written permission. There are knitwear designers who will design custom patterns for you to use at a very reasonable price. They know their yarns and can work out problems for you.

Wear you product, as this is one of the best advertisements there is and you will be surprised at the comments you receive.

BREEDING STOCK:

This is where you can make a profit with your business, but there are several criteria before you can become a successful breeder of quality goats.

Cashmere prices have fallen to a much more realistic price and this is encouraging more breeders into the market. This means that there is plenty of good quality stock available.

Firstly you must know enough about cashmere bearing goats to know what is good and what is not. Never sell an inferior goat for breeding purposes. If your sell bucks for pets you should neuter them before they leave your property. You never know if the buyer will use your animal for breeding and then start selling "cashmere goats" . You could lose your reputation as a reliable and ethical breeder.

Make sure your goats are healthy, free of parasites and if the prospective buyer wishes, vaccinated up to date. I do not sell animals for breeding purposes that are not vaccinated. There are blood screening tests you can do for certain diseases, such as C.A.E. (Caprine Arthritic Encephalitis) and C.L.A. (Caseous Lymphadenitis). Talk to your local veterinarian.

Make sure your buyer knows about cashmere goats and their specific needs, such as good fences. Make sure that they know that they can call on your for advice if they need to. I frequently help new goat breeders and everyone is happy with the arrangement. I know my goats are being well cared for.

Keep good accurate records on all of your animals. Tag and/or tatoo your breeding stock. CaPrA (Cashmere Producers of America) now has a Registration Program that is optional for breeders. Ear tag your kids soon after birth, in a few days they may begin to change colour and the does may even swap kids between them! This has happened to me more than once.

MEAT:

Goat meat is also know as chevon, this is supposed to enhance the image of the "lowly" goat. However, people from many countries in Europe, Asia and the Carribean have been eating goat meat for years and may be finding it difficult to obtain fresh meat locally. Advertise your product and soon you will have an established list of customers.

Eat the meat yourself and find out if you have a good product. You may be able to offer a few recipes for first time buyers.

Do not be discouraged if you do not make an instant profit. It takes time and hard work to get established, so make a five year plan and keep good accounts. Hopefully, you will soon be running an enjoyable and profitable business.

THE FUTURE OF CASHMERE

I am optimistic about the future of the cashmere industry in North America. There are recent changes in the economy that point to an increased interest in small businesses. Natural fibres are gaining in popularity, especially exotic fibres that can be grown locally. Designers, as well as spinners, weavers and knitters are more aware of the benefits of natural fibres and are more educated about them

One important reason for my optimism is the reasonable price for breeding stock, compared to really high prices a few years ago. This is bound to encourage greater numbers of people who are willing to take part in a relatively new industry. More people are now buying goats to raise meat, fibre and to use for weed control, instead of just being interested in raising breeding stock for sale.

North America needs more cashmere. We have been buying from other countries for many years because of the quality and availability of the product. Prices have been consistently lower for foreign fibres, but as North American producers gain more knowledge about the animals and cashmere, both the quality and quantity of the product will improve. Hopefully this will encourage consumers to buy North American cashmere.

Another very positive step is the fact that many producers have formed organizations, both regional, and national, to share information about the industry. These organizations are setting standards and educating the public as well as the producers, about cashmere goats and their fibre.

Raising cashmere bearing goats can be a profitable business and the future looks promising for those willing to face the challenge, and invest in this unique market.

GLOSSARY

Boer goats	originating in South Africa, may carry cashmere
britch	the rump area of the goat
Cashgora	a cross between an Angora goat and a cashmere bearing goat, a fibre that is too coarse to be considered cashmere
Combing	using a comb or small brush to remove fibre
Conformation	the shape and build of an animal
crimp	small waves in the fibre
culling	removing from the flock
dehairing	removing the hair fibres from the down fibres
down	the fine undercoat of the cashmere fleece
embryos	fertilized eggs
ennobled	improved
feral	wild
fleece	all the fibre on the animal
genes	factors that determine hereditary characteristics
guard hair	the outer coarse hair
hair follicles	cells that produce filaments of hair
hand/handle	the softness and feel of the fibre
homogenous blends	uniformly blended
intermediary fibre	a fibre with a diameter between that of down and hair
lustre	the sheen or silkiness of the fibre
medullated	hollow fibre
micron	unit of measurement, one millionth of a meter
minerals	an essential element of the dietary needs

mohair	the fleece of the Angora goat
moulting	shedding the fleece
nomads	wanderers
nubs	short pieces of fibre
pill	to form small balls of fibre on the garment
punis	a method of preparing fibre
rolags	prepared fibre for spinning
second cuts	short fibres made by passing the shears or clippers over an area of the animal twice
selenium	an essential mineral
shorn fleece	fleece removed by shears
underwool	down fibres
wheel ratio	the number of times the bobbin turns to each treadle
white muscle disease	a muscle weakness caused by insufficient Selenium
yield	the amount of fibre produced

BIBLIOGRAPHY

Baines, P. Spinning Wheels Spinners & Spinning. London, England: B.T. Batsford Ltd.1982 pp.199-201.

Barry, D.M. & Godke, R.A."Historical Development of the Boer Goat Breed", Fibre News, April/May 1994 pp.18-19.

Beattie, L. "Hunt Valley Cashmere" Brochure.

Cashmere America. "Fibre Classing and Clip Preparation Notes", Kiowa, Colorado.1993.

Davidson, Porter, Marguerite. A Handweaver's Pattern Book. Chester, Pa: John Spencer Inc.,pp.94.

Kilfoyle, S. Samson, L.B. Completely Angora. Brantford, Ontario: Samson Angoras. 2nd ed., pp 150-159.

Lupton, Dr. Christopher. "Characteristics of Goat Fibres", Cashmirror, Volume Six Issue Two, (November, 1994) pp.10-19.

Moorhouse, R. "The Future of New Zealand Cashgora", Fibre News, January, 1990 pp. 20-21.

Russel, A."Chinese Cashmere", Scottish Fibre News. June 1993 pp.4-5.

Ryder, M.L."Goat History", Fibre News, January, 1994 pp.18-19.

Stove, Margaret. M-E-R-I-N-O. Loveland, Colorado: Interweave Press,1991 pp.36-40.

CASHMERE RESOURCES

ORGANIZATIONS:

Cashmere Producers of America
P.O. Box 128
Menard, Texas
TX 76859

Eastern Cashmere Association
Tia Rosengarten
Box 37
Weston, Vermont
VT 05161

North West Cashmere Association
Gara Wegrich
5700 Demaray Dr.
Grant's Pass, Oregon
OR 97527

Texas Cashmere Association
Dr. Don Huss, President
P.O. Box 426
Menard, Texas
TX 76859

Cashmere America Co-Operative
P.O. Box 1126
Sonora, Texas
TX 76950

Professional Cashmere Marketer's Association Inc.
3299 Anderson Lane
Dillon, Montana
MT 59725

MAGAZINES

Concerning Cashmere
Newsletter of Cashmere Producers of America

Hoofprints
Newsletter of Eastern Cashmere Association

NWCA
Newsletter of North Western Cashmere Association

Cashmirror
P.O. Box 639
Toledo, Washington
WA 98591

INTERNET
Look up cashmere, goats and knitting and almost anything relating to fibre and you will find home pages on the World Wide Web (WWW) that deal with all these issues. Some of the resources and magazines listed here are also available through the Internet.

CASHMERE FIBRE AND YARNS

Canada
Sandy Pines Farm, R. R. #6 Napanee, Ontario. K7R 3L1

U.S.A.
Cashmere America, P.O. 1126, Sonora, TX. 76950

Bessey Place Cashmere, RD1, Buckfield, Maine. 04220

Rabbit Tree Farm, 130 Jack Road, Saxonburg, PA. 16056

Hunt Valley Cashmere, 6747 White Stone Road, Baltimore, Maryland. 21207.